ejo

The Felix Pollak Prize in Poetry
The University of Wisconsin Press Poetry Series
Ronald Wallace, General Editor

Now We're Getting Somewhere
David Clewell
Henry Taylor, Judge, 1994

The Legend of Light
Bob Hicok
Carolyn Kizer, Judge, 1995

Fragments in Us: Recent and Earlier Poems
Dennis Trudell
Philip Levine, Judge, 1996

Don't Explain
Betsy Sholl
Rita Dove, Judge, 1997

Mrs. Dumpty
Chana Bloch
Donald Hall, Judge, 1998

Liver
Charles Harper Webb
Robert Bly, Judge, 1999

Ejo: Poems, Rwanda, 1991–1994
Derick Burleson
Alicia Ostriker, Judge, 2000

ejo

POEMS
RWANDA
1991–1994

DERICK BURLESON

The University of Wisconsin Press

The University of Wisconsin Press
2537 Daniels Street
Madison, Wisconsin 53718

3 Henrietta Street
London WC2E 8LU, England

5   4   3   2   1

Printed in the United States of America

Library of Congress Cataloging-in-Publication Data

Burleson, Derick
Ejo : poems, Rwanda, 1991–1994/Derick Burleson.
pp. cm—(Felix Pollak prize in poetry)
ISBN 0-299-17020-9 (alk. paper)
ISBN 0-299-17024-1 (pbk. : alk. paper)
1. Rwanda—poetry. I. Title. II. Felix Pollak prize in poetry (Series)
PS3552.U7263 E36   2000
811'.6—dc21   00-010300

For Anita
And for Roger

Contents

Acknowledgments

Grateful acknowledgments to the following journals in which these poems first appeared.

Crab Orchard Review: "Bienvenue"

Cutbank: "Taxi"

The Georgia Review: "At the Border"

The Kenyon Review: "Umugabo Mukaga," "Good Customs"

Perihelion: "Remera Arrives," "Letter from Remera," "Remera's Story"

The Paris Review: "Ethnologist's Lament," "One Million One"

Monster: "Home Again"

Poetry: "Democracy," *"Ejo,"* "Howdy," "In This Country," "The Thief," *"Umuzungu Wambere* (First White Man)"

The Texas Review: "Letter to Remera in Rwanda," "Nyavirezi"

Western Humanities Review: "Curfew," "Waking Again"

I wish to thank the National Endowment for the Arts for support which enabled me to complete this book.

My gratitude to all who have read these poems and offered their suggestions and support.

ejo

Ejo

The Kinyarwandan word which means both yesterday and tomorrow

World resolves itself
in crowned crane's
liquid eye, in the cry

of ibis, eye that's gazed
on anyone who's ever walked
this path beneath acacias, through

coffee fields to the river
and back again carrying water or fish.
Cry that cries the morning news.

Come, let's walk this path
together, empty handed, carrying
nothing back but a few words

of a language powerful
enough to turn the river
back on itself, to fill the river

with bloated corpses.
One day I swam far
into Lake Kivu, a thousand

feet of clear water below
and nothing above except sun.
My body suspended on

surface tension, the line
between air and thicker air,
sun the point from which

the water swung. Yesterday
I swam. Now I'm back home.
Tomorrow Remera will swim

out into that same lake, almost
across the border, gut shot,
gasping, almost there, almost . . . .

Crowned crane wears
a slash of crimson at the throat.
Beneath its golden crest, beneath

its liquid eye, the path winds
through coffee fields
to the river and back again.

Fathom yourself in exile.
In every gurgle of each
morning's pot of coffee

you hear your brother's last
breath. You wake in a forest.
You've been shot. Get up,

stagger down the path
to the river full of corpses.
In its ancient terrible cry

(fling your body in)
ibis pronounces how
beginning becomes the end.

I

Imana yirwa ahandi igataha i Rwanda.
(God spends the day somewhere else but comes
home to sleep in Rwanda.)

Howdy

And then they were all staring at me.
So I shout: This is a typical American greeting.
C'est une salutation typiquement Américaine.

Please understand, this is the first day of school
and the year before, there was no school
because of the war, *une année blanche*, a white year,

a blank year, and school was supposed to start
in September and it's October already, the first day
of school a month late, just when we've all begun

to wonder if school would start this year or not.
123 unpronounceable names, every first-year
pre-med student in Rwanda gathered here in this room

to learn from me all the English they'd ever need:
If a bomb went off it would be really tragic.
They throw wads of notepaper, gyrate their hips,

sing *Mama We!*, whistle, sprint up and down the aisles,
leap from seat to plastic seat. I stumble down
each concrete step to the auditorium's bowels

as if I were descending the icy rungs of hell,
and they shriek at me in a language I can't understand:
Umuzungu urashaka iki? Umuzungu subira iwanyu!

White man what do you want? White man go home!
The microphone's stainless steel lung looks like
something with which to club them into submission.

So I rear back and holler Howdy, sheer horror
takin' me back to that Oklahoma twang I thought
I'd done gone and give up fer good. And when

they holler back: How-Dee, it's an amazing grace.
So I do it again and so do they. All semester I howl
English and they bellow it back, the future doctors

of Rwanda chanting in unison: shinbone connected
to the kneebone, kneebone connected to the hipbone.
And by December when I meet them between classes

under the blossoms of the campus poinsettia, I say
Muraho and they say How-dee. I say *Amakuru* and they ask
How're ya'll doin? I say *Nimeza* and they say Jes fine.

Good Customs

If you have a sweet potato, give half to your brother.
Before serving guests a gourd of *urwagwa*,
sip through the straw yourself to show it's not poisoned.

When you meet your neighbor in the market
shake hands and exclaim, "You're still alive!"
Wish him large herds when you part.

When you plan to marry, present your future father
with a hoe and a cow. Before bedding your husband,
leave a pitcher of water for Lyangombe, goddess

of fecundity, since there's no greater sadness
than dying with no grandchildren to mourn you.
It's futile to fight the will of Imana.

You're rubbed twice with butter: Once when you're born.
Once when you die. Bury your first child's placenta
under the bed. Wrap the umbilical cord into an amulet.

When you need to know the future, take a bottle full
of your own spit to the *umupfumu*, and he'll fry it
to read the spirits' will. If a wife whistles,

her husband is doomed. When someone sneezes say,
"Be rich." They'll answer, "Together." Harvest
bananas before they ripen or crows will eat them all.

Attend Mass each Sunday. When you get home,
sacrifice butter and beer at the ancestors' altars.
Let only laughter scar your face.

Taxi

Doorman slams the sliding door, yells go
HurryHurryHurry, cursing the ancient
battered Toyota minibus, cursing God,
the gravel in the gearbox, Driver,
the soldiers at the next checkpoint,
the choking six-cylinder, the president,
the bald tires, the dangerous curves,
the sun that rose not long ago: StopStopStopStop
he screams and Driver does his best to cram
the brake pedal through what's left of the floorboards.
Doorman slams open the door and smiles
and swings his arm wide in welcome.

This is where we get on
and take the last places in the back
on a leopard-print Naugahyde seat
we have to ourselves. Good Morning,
a man smiles. *Mwaramutse ho,* I answer.
Imana bless us, Driver says,
Truly the world's coming to an end.
My brother speaks their language
and the *umuzungu* speaks ours.
Doorman yells *TugendeTugende*
and we go, Bob Marley on the radio jammin'
I need a hamma, a hamma, a hamma to hamma them down.

And even the soldiers smile and wave
us through the barricade as we head out
of town, Driver hunched over the wheel,
begging the engine for speed, racing
all the other taxis north to the capital,
gaining altitude, the carburetor wheezing

like an asthmatic cow. We open the window
for a little air and the woman in front
shuts it. We open it. She shuts it.
Wind gives you malaria, she says.
Mosquitoes give you malaria, we say,
but this time the window stays shut.

Driver pulls us onto the shoulder
and Doorman grates open the door
for a family traveling to a wedding,
the mothers wearing their hair bound
up under strips of bamboo, their three
brightest cloths wrapped tight.
Then we're wedged together,
brothers and sisters and children
all sharing rivers of sweat.
The bridesmaid hands us a basket
finely woven of turquoise and purple
to save it from being crushed.

We pass on hills, pass on curves,
pass more battered taxis, trucks
hauling green bananas and sacks of beans,
women with hoes over their shoulders,
men walking to visit their neighbors,
carrying gourds of banana beer,
squads of soldiers marching to the border,
a bicycle so strung with live chickens
the rider seems to be pedaling
dinner for the whole army.
Driver skids us around another blind corner
and now the taxi's a sauna,

with every breath we breathe human,
smiling, trading handshakes,

even though we all know
that when they demand our identity cards
at the next checkpoint, the soldiers'
Kalichniokavs will be loaded,
that the basket I'm holding could
have a grenade inside, that wired beneath
the 100-franc bill six schoolchildren
cluster around in the playground
across the road, there is almost certainly
a landmine.

Hardware Man

Lordly in aspect, yet
what an assortment
he wears on his chest:
a fan-belt bandolier
dangling springs and pistons,

valves, brake shoes, screws,
nuts and bolts, a battered pot,
serving spoons and knives all
pilfered from La Sympathique
where he dines each day for free.

He sleeps outside the market.
Whatever you want, he's got,
but none of it's for sale.
He's *fou*, Remera tells us.
The gendarmes lock him up

de temps en temps. Years
of bearing this load have
turned his thighs to iron,
a 21st Century Man, half
his body gleams, holy,

a King to rule what's coming.
His crown an empty Omo box,
eucalyptus branch for a scepter,
he catches me staring, clanks over.
His scepter whips down.

I am knighted.

Bienvenue

It's the Fourth of July
and getting hotter in this tiny country
made famous by Dian Fossey

and a mountain gorilla she named Digit.
The whole crowd's standing on the middle
tier of the American ambassador's triple-

terraced lawn, which is painfully green
and leads up to the back porch of his Georgian
mansion. Nearby, a Rwandan man in high-collared linen

serves ice-cold Coca-Cola in plastic cups.

Anybody who's everybody's here:
Isn't that the minister of information? the AIDS researcher
from San Francisco whispers.

Then gossip turns to the ambassador's wife's school,
her plans to level the lawn and install a swimming pool,
olympic-sized. The cultural attaché's sweating bullets. *Bienvenue,*

Welcome. The loudspeaker squeals a flash of feedback.

Dinner, McDonald's hamburgers flown fresh from Belgium,
is served and soon yellow paper wrappers litter the lawn.
President Habyarimana arrives looking pretty calm

considering his country's embroiled in civil war.
He accepts the Coke offered by the ambassador
as Boy Scouts from both nations flag-salute Rwanda's proud *R*

and the Stars and Stripes writhing like cobras together.

Visiting Supreme Court Justice Sandra Day O'Connor
orates in French tattered as a poached lion's mane of honor.

The crowd applauds and bright fireworks shed petals
from heaven as the soldiers of the Rwandan National
Band, who've been standing stiff and proud at attention all

evening slip into a hip-hop rendition of the "Star-Spangled Banner."

Umuzungu Wambere (First White Man)
Count Von Götzen, 1894

When the man with no skin
came over the hill, I said
to my brother: Hey. Look there.
That man has no skin. The man
walked closer. He raised his arms
in the air. He came closer still.

My brother said to me: No. I think
he has skin. But it's bright red.
Doesn't look like skin to me, I said.
We saw little suns where his eyes
should be, the tortoise shell perched
on his head, saw that he had no toes

but walked on brown stumps instead.
Hi, said the man with no skin,
How's the news? Hi, we said.
The news is good, we said.
I come from far away, he said.
There are many more like me.

I want to see the King, he said.
We laughed. He couldn't speak very well,
this man with no skin. Nobody sees the King.
We laughed again and ran through the city,
shouting the news as we went.
The man with no skin wants to see the King!

He wants to see the King!
Nobody sees the King.
People sprinted from their houses.
Torture him! Kill him! they shouted.

He wants to see the King!
String him up! Poke him with spears!

But he followed us to the palace,
too stupid to be scared,
and all the people followed him,
the bright red man with no skin.
Nobody killed him.
And that was our first mistake.

Nyavirezi

Nyavirezi loved walking.
Every day she stretched her legs
across the acacia-scattered savanna
or beneath the rainforest's
giant ferns, along Rift Valley lakeshores
or riverbanks she could follow
north to the Nile. Up volcanoes' steep

green slopes, pushing through stands
of giant lobelia, until she reached
the summit of Karisimbi, the grandfather,
or Bisoke to swim all afternoon
in the sacred lake at crater's center.
She walked to measure the kingdom.
She walked for the pleasure of walking.

Then one dry season at the hour trees
throw no shade and her shadow
disappeared, Nyavirezi felt thirsty.
But the only water she found
was a puddle in a thorn tree's hollow stump.
It didn't quench her thirst.
It was lion piss.

Striding back home through tall grass
that evening Nyavirezi spied
her father's long-horned cows
and felt wind gust through
her head. She shivered once,
sprouted tawny fur and claws
and glinting fangs. She caught a calf,

broke its neck, and ate it
hide and bones and all. Then she changed
back into a smooth-skinned woman again.
Her brother began to notice more calves
missing from the herd, found the lion tracks.
He took his spear, watched from the moonlit hill,
and saw Nyavirezi shiver and change. He told their father,

who forbade Nyavirezi ever to leave
the family compound again. But a young prince
came courting, driving eleven young cows
with sweeping horns. Her father said, "Love your husband,
but never tell your secret." So she married and soon
gave birth to a girl-child she called Nyavirungu,
daughter of volcanoes. Her husband heard

the servants whisper: "Well at least
she doesn't have claws and teeth."
He snatched his spear, ran to Nyavirezi's room
and demanded to know her secret. So she shivered once,
killed him, ate him, then took up her daughter,
and went home to her father. Nyavirezi was beautiful.
Be careful what you wish for.

Hunger, Beard, and the Man

"I'm hungry," says Hunger.
"Can you help me out
for some bananas and beans?
I'll pay you back soon."
Beard knew there'd be trouble,
but who can refuse a friend,
the brother you choose?
And they were friends.
Beard remembered all those good times,
running through the tea fields of their youth.

"OK," he says. "I'll lend you the money.
What are friends for?"
Then Hunger grew happy.
He knew Beard would help him out.
And truly, he has only the best intentions
as he takes the money and buys
the best calabash of *urgwagwa* he can find.
He toasts Beard many times through
that warm afternoon of bliss.
You can't blame Hunger for being what he is.

Time passes, each day a happy twin
of the day before. All this while
Beard is missing his money.
Why oh why did he ever loan Hunger that cash?
I remember all those nights Mother told us
this story, how angry I was at Hunger.
How could he betray his friend?
And then, when Beard finally comes knocking,
how happily I awaited what comes next,
how Hunger talks sweet: "Come back

tomorrow. I'll have your money by then."
We know Hunger is lying.
But Beard goes back home and we groan,
knowing that when he returns tomorrow,
Hunger still will not have the money,
knowing Beard will grow angry
and take his machete, knowing how Hunger
must flee for his life down the long path
from hilltop to river and back again.
Man now enters the story,

and (unlucky for us!) stops to see
what's the trouble. Along comes Hunger
screaming, "Help me! Help me! *Aidez moi!*"
When Man opens his mouth in surprise,
in leaps Hunger. But when Beard tries
to follow, Man slams it shut again.
That is why Man carries Beard on his face,
why he suffers the agonies of Hunger,
why everywhere Man travels,
he carries a machete.

Ethnologist's Lament

All day I measure noses.
People are brought before me.
My brass calipers never lie.

If the nose is long enough,
I give that person a card.
If not, I shrug and smile.

I keep meticulous records.
Research shows self is a science.
The laws of Nature are exact.

The sun is savage here,
burns my nose quite raw.
I haven't caught the brain fever

yet, though many have. A few
even died. The women here
are lovely. I shouldn't say so.

The noses of Tutsis are identical
to ours. Outrage! you cry.
Color is the only difference.

I can show you my records.
I wonder how you'd measure up.
We know now the length of nose

is a sign of the finer perceptions
noble blood bestows. Our card
shows those capable to receive

those gifts we bring, gifts of God
and science to create, we anticipate,
an oasis of advanced civilization

here beneath this savage sun.
Yet my work is full of sorrow.
I pity those Hutus whose noses

are only almost long enough.
The laws of Nature never lie.
My brass calipers are quite exact.

I work for the good of my king.
I work for the good of our colony,
beautiful among a thousand hills.

I miss my wife back home.
My work is full of sorrow.
So few noses are long enough.

The sun rises and sets at six.
All night I dream of noses.
Noses just too short

to learn the laws of God
and science. I wear a helmet
against the sun.

The Thief

Rudely interrupting my lecture on Derrida:
a chatter of machine-gun fire: dada dada da.

Eyes suddenly wide, my students and I
duck and hunker down by our desks, sign

and signified forgotten in a flutter of abandoned texts,
figuring the long-rumored attack is on at last.

Etienne gets brave enough to peek out the window
and ask the uniforms he sees gathered below

just what in the hell's going on. When it turns
out to be merely a thief they've shot in a corner

of the vacant classroom next door, we all spill
outside laughing, a little sheepish at that strange thrill

we'd felt: how war engenders a sort of relief.
We gather in a semicircle and watch gendarmes drag the thief,

dirty and bleeding, from his niche of hiding,
arms bound tight behind his back. There was nothing

to do now but return to our books (since all the fun
was over), so that I might, again, explain deconstruction.

In This Country

So you've come into this country
searching for what? Not the diamonds
of *King Solomon's Mines* or even
Gorillas in the Mist. But every
morning when you wake, the romantic
volcanoes you hope stay extinct
are just another adventure waiting

to greet you when you kiss your wife
Stewart Granger–style goodbye
and sail off to teach *Moby Dick*
to students who already speak
three other languages and play
basketball in the afternoons.
Equatorial mornings and nights

drip regular as the faucet
in the indoor bathroom you never
dreamed you'd have, and rains
rise and fall with the rhythm
of love. Circles and cycles, all
Newton's heavenly bodies hug the earth
in this country where *ejo* means

both yesterday and tomorrow and your skin
turns dark as strong tea. *Mwaramutse*,
the word for Good Morning sticks
like honey in your throat each day,
and the passion fruit you eat for breakfast
tastes multisyllabic as its name, *intababara*.
Untranslatable, landlocked, what is whale?

Why catch it? What is the significance of white?
Queequeg guards your house with a machete
each night, and before you sleep, you kill
the mosquitoes which used to be as big
as elephants, the story goes, until they learned
to drink *urwagwa*, the bittersweet banana beer.
At least *imodoka* means Toyota in this country

where malaria is more common than the cold,
the colonial rose gardens brighter than stoplights.
And even in the rainy season, with all its fevered
nights, you wear nothing to bed and dream
Lawrence of Arabia in the language you learn
little by little like the bird builds its nest:
Ndashaka, I want. *Amazi*, water.

II

Ibye ejo bibara abejo.
(The things of tomorrow will be recounted
by the people of tomorrow.)

Beasts

I. Giant Cockroach

Having had enough of their tribe, I snatched
the yellow can labeled Hatari from the very back
of the kitchen cupboard. *Hatari* means danger
in Kiswahili. One too many holes had appeared
in the plastic bags of sugar—roach mandibles
like Swiss Army knife scissors, snip, snip.
Oh, they'd watched me watch them one too many
times, insolently cleaning their faces.
They'd built empires somehow inside our bedroom's
concrete walls, and at night we could hear them
there, hear them in the ceiling tiles.
While we slept, their six-hinged scabblings
crept into our dreams. How many generations?
Denizens of the corner, armored as tanks,
shiny carapace, trembling antennae. Stomp
them hard enough, they pop. You have to love
their ability to survive. I'd avoided that Hatari
can for months, scared of what it might contain.
But when I drank a roach drowned in my Coke
in the middle of the night, I sprayed my enemies
with all the danger there was, more casualties
than I cared to count helpless on their backs,
frantically treading six new trenches
in the poison air—then stumbled back to bed,
sick of belly, dizzy of head, glad at heart.

II. Giant Earthworm

Bigger around than your thumb, longer
than your forearm, it barricades our path
through Nyungwe Forest. Nile perch dream
all their lives of worms like this.
I thought at first Snake! and Adam's apple
fluttered my throat. The worm's tunnel
leads down through liana stems, through
the root filaments of giant ferns, down
into the other rainforest beneath our feet.
Rain mists breathing leaves, layers
of fallen leaves, black loam and rot,
to the very tip of the farthest root,
moistening so the tumescent worm can glide
along the forest floor, each concentric ring
contracting to move it toward its mate who even now
sings a Siren song in the silent language
of worms. One end is male, the other female,
so it doesn't matter how they meet.
Imagine their children! Everything's large
here, too large, and we know this royalty of worms
will rule long after we've hiked back
to the highway and hitched a ride home.
"Leave it alone," says my wife. "Poor thing."
I pick it up to prove I can, then let it go.

III. Chiggo

With a formidably sharp knife,
my angelic wife digs a hole
in my big toe, carving *buhoro, buhoro*
through the callus grown hiking
daily kilometers in Birkenstocks.
Mark but this chiggo!
Sure, there's blood involved,
but unlike Donne's flea,
our blood's not in the chiggo,
the chiggo's in me.
And so is Anita, digging
ever deeper with her bright
stainless steel, trying
to locate the source of my pain.
Chiggo lurks in greenest
grass and awaits the chance
to launch herself and cling, unseen,
unfelt, insinuating into hapless
hosts who have no choice
but to receive this unwelcome guest,
a second cousin come to drink
all the beer. Insidious as radio
politics, chiggo burrows in
and lays eggs so her darlings
can hatch and feed, feed and grow.
When my wife has dug deep enough,
ah, the white explosion when she
squeezes my big toe with love enough
to force chiggo and chiggo-spawn
back into the blank inhospitable world.

IV. Chameleon

We're at the neighbors' naming,
and now the baby's named, so we drag
our chairs and our beers out front,
all us men, while the women
tidy up inside. We're chatting
de tout et de rien, and then someone
spots a chameleon crossing the hard-packed
compound, twitching like God's marionette
or a wind-up toy made in its own image,
carved from the finest tropical hardwood,
each tiny scale painted tea-plantation green.
Black eyes mere pinpricks, one looks forward
while the other watches the trail behind.
Tail coiled up out of the way, his forehead
sports three horns which make him look scarier
than he really is. He's all loose hinges, old door,
and slow, slow except for his tongue,
which he can flick like a bullwhip
dipped in honey and snap a damselfly
from the air. We watch a while
longer before my neighbor leans over
and whispers conspiratorially:
"*Witonde sha!* If he bites you,
you'll become a woman."

V. Mountain Gorilla

When the silverback screams and charges,
his mouth all yellow molars and nettles,
I marvel how easily I've assumed
(just as the guide demonstrated we should)
the submissive posture, cowering flat
on my belly, flared nostrils full
of primate musk and rainforest loam.
We've hiked an hour through this Tarzan movie,
our guide flicking his shiny machete
to prune the occasional frond sprouted
since he last came this way, leading
another dozen tourists to the shady
hillside where he guesses the gorillas
will feed today. His part performed,
the silverback withdraws into the brush,
strikes the pose of Rodin's Thinker,
and rests his massive chin on a fist
vast as a linebacker's helmeted head,
bored by this daily hour when the smelly
hairless cousins come to visit.
We remember our cameras (flashes off),
now that we've begun to breathe again.
The silverback sulks and his six wives
placidly return to eating and grooming
and nursing their young, the pregnant one
leaning back in a patch of sun, rubbing
the sunshine over her belly. Clickety-click
our cameras chorus, click, click, click.
Right on cue, the youngest son shinnies
up a tree and hangs from one hand,

beating his chest hard with the other.
Our guide smiles at us and beats his chest.
The dangling child drums his some more, then
all of us beat our chests in unison,
while the silverback knits his brows
over this daily silliness he must endure.

Umugabo Mukaga

Here's a man with a problem:

Beneath the branch from which he dangles,
        a crocodile roaring in the river.

Beside the ax he forgot in his wild scramble skyward,
        a lion snarling open-mouthed.

Coiled around his branch and slithering closer,
        a reticulated python ready to constrict.

Their terrible fangs are needle sharp.
        They're large and really ravenous.

Our friend came here to cut down the tree,
        to fetch some wood for his wife

who still waits at home to build a supper fire
        for sweet potatoes and the beans.

He can't force himself to let go of the branch
        clutched tight in both hands,

can't swim away in the river. Crocodile is hungry.
        Can't shinny down the tree.

Lion is hungry. Can't stay where he is any longer.
        Python creeps closer.

He's already hacked a good notch and now
        the acacia is beginning to teeter.

Our friend's *umugabo mukaga,* up the creek, we'd say.
And though he hasn't realized it yet,

that other man sipping beer at the table beneath this mural,
waiting for his friends to arrive,

fingering his machete, wondering if it's sharp enough . . .
he's going to have a big problem too.

Abazungu

I. Getting There

Children again when we step off
the plane, we can't believe
how direct the sun, how short
our shadows have become.
Cold orange Fantas a schoolboy sells
from his ice-filled tin bucket cost
just a quarter. A soldier stamps
our passports at the border,
and the first Rwandans we see
flash down the hill chiming their bicycle bell:
Wake up! Watch out! A bunch of green
bananas tied to the rack, mother
and child balance on handlebars,
precarious as cease-fires.
Our English worthless in this new country,
we *Ça va?* each other before passion-fruit
breakfast, then trundle off to class,
arms loaded with books, *les bons mots*
they say we'll need in the market.
Dinner in *le réfectoire*: strange fish
we can't name any more, then off to bed,
tossing all night in humid dreams,
two cots shoved together, swaddled apart
by mosquito nets. Out the window,
Lake Kivu kisses the same beach it's kissed
a million years now, and fishermen chant songs
old as water to haul their nets
through the silver schools.

II. The Source

Today dawns dim and we emerge
naked into waist-high ferns,
bathe in the brisk waterfall,
glance back and notice how
our bright blue nylon bower
seems to draw the rainforest
up around it. Later, a Batwa man
lopes down the trail, pauses to stare,
aghast at the complexities *abazungu*
need to survive. Deep in the eternal
shade of mahogany trees, we sight
orchids, the pale and sometimes
carnivorous flower which thrives
in low light. If only Livingstone
had made it this far upcountry,
discovered this hidden source
and then died, how many millions
could have stayed home? Tomorrow
or the next day we'll backpack down
into the valley, pay a guide five dollars
to hack a path through the jungle
to where the fabled spring boils up
from beneath, and feel a little born again
when we kneel to drink.

III. Trash

Victims of packaging here
where there is no garbageman,
we ask Joseph, nightguard and gardener,
what to do. For compost, we all agree,
a pit beneath the banana tree.
Burn the rest, he says. So into the fire
go our students' first essays in English.
We save all the glass for the bottle man
who comes collecting once a week,
and Joseph winds plastic bags into
a ball for his nine children to kick.
Soon crows learn where to find
hamburger scraps, circling the house
each day after lunch. Joseph keeps
the Cheetos canister our folks mailed
from home to store garden seeds.
Finally there remains only the problem
of complicated medicines: the foil
and plastic bubblepacks our antimalarials
come in just won't burn. Then one day
we find Joseph studying the dense
French instruction pamphlet that comes
with each and every moon's
worth of birth control pills.

IV. Charity

Outside the *boulangerie*, a kilo
of beef bumping in my backpack,
we face off with a baker's dozen
beggars gathered in an arc
to block our way. Hands held out,
palms cupped, everybody's missing
something: an arm here, a leg there.
Then a mother pushes through the crowd
gripping her child like a plow,
their clothes twisted generations
of hand-me-downs the color
of dry-season dust. She shifts her grip,
pries open the boy's lips: new teeth
already rotten to the gums. When we try
to shove past, she steps in front again,
demands that we pay. But we've had practice
with this sort of thing, have agreed
to give at the post office and nowhere else.
So we press on, change jingling
in our blue-jean pockets, straddle
our mountain bikes and pedal home,
dust and dead skin cells swirling
a precise accounting in our wake.

V. Attack

First thing we know
a friend's pounding at the door
saying, Hey, come on. There's a war
going on out here! It's the middle
of the night and sure enough
the syntax of attack sounds real close:
machine-gun ellipses, exclamations
of mortar shells. All the neighbors
gather outside, voices slung low,
as if guns had ears. The fireworks
go on until first light, when we think
the sunbirds will sing as usual,
the rebel army will retreat
over the volcanoes like it has before.
But when a government soldier
comes limping gunshot up the road,
we shoulder our backpacks,
and, never having been refugees before,
join our friends, no, join
the whole countryside carrying
whatever's too important to leave behind:
a baby pig, the Singer sewing machine,
a broken camera that will never
take snapshots again.

VI. Hostages

I feel like talking, Ntihinyuzwa says
somewhere in the middle of those dark
twelve hours when we'd given up hope
of rescue for the night. Behind us
in the schoolbus thirty other students
and their teachers mumble or sleep,
plumping their thrown-together bags
of clothes for pillows. We three lean
together around the gearshift knob
as if it's a campfire and say the poems
or parts of poems we can remember:
Let us go then you and I while the evening
is turning and turning in the widening gyre
the falcon gets lost the center cannot hold
I should have been a pair of ragged claws
the blood-dimmed tide is loosed I heard
a fly buzz tattered clothes upon a stick
to say I am Lazarus come back from the dead
to tell you all I shall tell you all.
Ntihinyuzwa teaches American Literature
at the university. The hills around here
are very gothic, he says, just like in Poe.
We've all heard rumors of massacre
in this village. And what a great story
this will make, he says, if we live
to tell it. Bus windows fogged, the season
drizzles into itself and every so often outside
another ancestor saunters by.

III

Urupfu rurarya ntiruhaga.
(Death eats and is never full.)

Democracy

Here it's the rainy season, but it still hasn't rained
so there's nothing for the dusty woman
in the roadside field to do but lean
on her hoe as if it's become a part of her body

and watch the bored checkpoint soldier
ask the suited and tied businessman
for the identity card he can't seem to find.
Unconcerned, the Mercedes Benz pants in the heat,

the soldier just wants a cold beer,
the woman would rather be planting her beans,
and the businessman, who's obviously from the wrong tribe,
keeps sweating and praying that the magic card

will materialize in some inside jacket pocket.
And if a tourist had snapped a photo of them all
like this, had in the instant stolen the souls
from this frightened man, this half-smiling woman,

the soldier just beginning to swing his gun around,
anybody with eyes in their heads
would still swear years later
something was bound to happen soon.

La Sympathique

Elbows propped, we lean in
around our platter, spooning
tomatoes and sauce thick with peanut flour,
onions, two chickens, a sheaf of green bananas,

sipping Primus beer. It's so good,
igisafuriya—enough to feed the whole army
we laugh, Rwagasana and Ulali and Anita and me.
A tethered goat bleats outside the kitchen.

Our waiter chases a barefoot beggar
away with a stick. Two crows
peck through the garbage heap.
Rwagasana and Ulali graduated from Stanford

where they learned to speak American.
I ask how would you say *igisafuriya*.
He says casserole or maybe stew.
Rwagasana and Ulali live next door.

They're so happy we're here,
we eat at their house every day.
Friday afternoons, we all come to town,
our favorite cafe: La Sympathique.

It's the rainy season and thunderheads
cut us some shade. A man stumbles in wearing
a 100-kilo sack of potatoes like a helmet.
Eucalyptus smoke spirals up from the *imbabura*.
A soldier strolls over to say *Muraho*
and shakes hands all around. Have some, we say.
He lays his rifle across another table,

grabs a spoon, digs in.

A machete of lightning, then rain drums
communiqués across the tin roof.
We scoot closer to keep our backs dry,
look up and smile through steam still

rising from our food. It's so good
we keep at it until
even the soldier
leans back and groans *ndahaze.*

Mango

Some people can't eat
them at all: an allergy
that cracks and swells
tongue   lips   cheeks
until it's hard to breathe.
Mango rot, they call it.

(I never would have believed
anything could be sweeter
than a tree-ripened peach.)

Even beneath the tough
red and green mottled skin
it's still not all nectar
and light: a large fibrous pit,
overripe and sticky strings
get caught in your teeth.

(No travel guide says how sharp
morning smoke smells rising
from valleys like hope.)

I like them green with lime juice
and *pili pili*. It's best to know
the price before you barter
in the market. The biggest varieties
ripen into two hemispheres
like a planet, or a heart.

(I wonder what's become
of the thin-featured woman
who sold bright fruit door to door.)

On the dusty, endless train
from Arusha to Dar es Salaam, escaping
civil war, we ate mango after mango
to save our souls. Mount Meru
wavered, a half-glimpsed god
drowsing across savannas of heat:

Mangoes   diamonds   bullets
if I had two, I'd give one to you.

Umwami in the Museum
Umwami Cyirima II Rujugiro, d.1708

O King, not quite three centuries and now your kingdom
has come to this: A glass case, your bones
more or less arranged in proper order, brass and iron
bracelets, your amulets, quartz crystals scattered
from volcanoes, blue beads fallen from your crown.

Should we thank the archeologists who unearthed
sacred drums, racks of spears and clubs, bows and arrows?
Or the courtiers who dried your body over holy fire,
wrapped you in a bull's hide, planted the acacia grove
above your grave? Curators arranged your skull so you stare

past the row of photographs, your descendants' souls stolen
by the *abazungu's* glass eye: *Intore,* white headdresses frozen
wild in dance, the royal herd of cows on parade, wide horns
gilded, strands of blue beads draped over their polls,
high jumpers eternally suspended above the helmeted heads

of bespectacled Belgian colonists, notebooks in hand.
The holes that held your eyes still stare past the faded
daguerreotypes framing the soothsayer rapt over the boiling
water and a ball of butter just dropped in to tell
the future, your future O Umwami, your people's . . . .

Your empty sockets still stare past rows of baskets
and milk pots and calabashes for beer, past the replica
of your thatch palace, past the porch and woven mats
and stools set out for the coterie when your poets sang
your praises and the bounty of the land. Your poets

are dead, King, and you cannot turn your head,
cannot turn your eyeless skull away from prophecy:
your tribe's corpses floating the Nile north to Egypt,
the land too dry for grass now, the cows too thin
to give any milk to mix with all the blood.

Curfew

In the cone of the headlights of the last
taxi-bus home from Ruhengeri, a family hustles
down the macadam, great-aunts and second cousins

and neighbors, at least a hundred bare feet
callused by years of walking pumice hills
slapping asphalt. Night punches through sky

like an obsidian fist, and it's past time to be home.
In the middle of the group in the middle of the road,
strung between two poles, a bamboo basket,

the kind they weave here to carry the sick or dead.
Three men shoulder it on each side, striding
in unison so their burden barely bounces,

and in the dazzle of headlights we see their relative
has become an ancestor, already cocooned
in old blankets. They've come from the hospital

in town. Picture them there, gathered
around the cot where this failing grandfather
has already divided the land among six sons.

Stubborn as mahogany root, he refuses
to submit until sundown. They shuffle
their feet, glance at the dimming window,

and wish he'd hurry up and die. A year
from now they'll use hoes and machetes
to harvest their neighbors' heads

then flee across the border to refugee camps
rampant with cholera. Outside the hospital window,
soldiers drunk on an afternoon's free beer

man their posts, ready to kill anyone out too late.
This is how they live in war. Beans have been planted,
and market day is still market day. But they must

carry their ancestor home at a run:
the women will wash the body all night
and shave their heads and keen. Outside

the teeth of men around the fire gleam
as calabashes of *urwagwa* pass,
and the cows of the dead are counted.

Glass Tower

Build in your mind a room
and fill it with people.
Take ten rooms full of people

and put them all in a gymnasium,
a gymnasium built of glass.
Stack 100 glass gymnasiums

each on top of the other
and in each room in each gymnasium
all the people doing different things:

a party, music, everyone's dancing,
cooking rooms and eating rooms,
rooms for drinking banana beer,

a market where you bargain
for papayas and mangoes, for tea
and tobacco and used shoes,

a pasture full of goats and cows,
a church to pray in, a soccer game,
rooms for telling long stories,

a wedding, a birth, a naming, a funeral,
a rainforest of ferns and mahogany trees
and lianas, rivers meandering through

savannas north to the Nile, fishermen
casting nets in those rivers,
pregnant women hoeing green fields

of beans and maize and potatoes,
and stairs so we can walk where
we want. The whole world can see in.

It's beautiful, it glitters in the sun
this architectural miracle built all
of glass. Outside, a pyramid of stones.

At the Border

a pile of machetes and hoes
higher than your head   most bloodstained

and every thirty seconds or so
another body pounds
down Rusumo Falls   in the pool
at the bottom they bob
back and forth so
bloated and gray
you might think
massacre had created

                        a new race

beyond the border   those farmers
who piled these tools of food and war
sit for days waiting for a kilo of beans
the rains begin again   it's that time of year

nobody drinks from the river

on land the bodies
seem wings of laundry
bright cloth spread
on the Akagera bank
to dry   flat as if
the flesh inside
were already sinking

                    eager for the river

in the water these pale balloons
float easily
north to Lake Victoria

so putrid even crocodiles

                             stay away

behind the border every day
while the gods hover like starving birds
Achilles still pursues Hector
round the city walls
and makes very sure
when he catches up   he waits
long enough
to hear the voice pleading
before he swings the blade

Home Again

April Fool's and snow
the day we come back to ourselves
in the Safeway cereal aisle.
Frosted Flakes, Lucky Charms,

we can't seem to choose among
all the air-conditioned colors
of boxes shelved under lights
designed to make them glow.

We've learned again how
to accelerate through rush-hour
traffic down Kansas City freeways,
crossing the Missouri each day

into the neighboring state.
Safe at home we eat fast food
each night and channel-surf
until sleep takes us on the sofa,

blue tides of TV light lapping
our knees. Then one morning
we wake to our local newsman saying
President Habyarimana's plane

is still in flames on the runway,
and all the next month we watch
as our friends are murdered,
or murder.

Letter to Remera in Rwanda

Since we know by now
you're probably already dead,
your sisters and brothers are dead,
your mother and father, aunts and uncles are dead,
your rotting corpses and twenty thousand others
clotting the air down the hilly streets of Nyamirambo,
I'll keep this short.

We hoped you'd remember us
as we remember you, our two years
together: that day we met in Bukavu
and you told us our French was *mauvais* (we could barely say
je ne comprends pas), how you couldn't think of leaving
us alone for our first anniversary. *Tous seuls?*
We keep your photo on the fridge.

Maybe you're still alive.
We know you're smart and lucky,
but the *amakuru* we see on CNN, a man
who slashes his neighbor, bends to check,
then slashes again, piles of dead women still wrapped
in bright *pagnes*, flies laying eggs in their eyes,
how could this happen *chez vous*

where we all danced away New Year's Eve together?
Umwaka mwiza the whole town shouted at midnight.
Buhoro, buhoro ni rwo urugendo, little by little,
the bird builds its nest. We've heard stories from those
who escaped, how they hid beneath their mothers' bodies
until the army rumbled off to kill another town.
Just hoping you're one of them.

Letter from Remera

In first let me wish you all things, the best are peace.
It is difficult to start this letter because I don't know what plus to say.
All the news are very horrible.
My friends, my brothers, and my parents no longer are.
My papa a *étè tuer,* my brother Remy also was killed in Butare.
Maman stays in Kigali without the spirit to revive.
And me, I received bullets, but the wounds seem in good health.
Mes amis: Clément is dead.
Phillipe and Fulgence have disappeared.
Vianney is found in Cyangugu.
Let me make you believe that right now, here, nothing goes.
For the moment I am in shock and nobody is capable of giving me
    back my smile.
The world is showing me its evil face.
Can you imagine such a chronology of evil things on one lone person?
There are insecurities all over the country.
I am incapable of helping survive my family.
Some people search always to put an end to the lives of others.
My day-after-tomorrow is incertain and so it is hard to tell you of
    my future projects.
I live under the love of heaven and that from day to day.
Only this: one day we will see each other again in the world if you
    are still believers.
May *Dieu* protect us. Hope you all best things are Peace.

One Million One

Refugees flee their homes. Exiles
move back in, thirty-year echoes
of mortar shells rattling windows.

> Down the river bloated bodies bob.
> Little Brother, which body is yours?

Relief planes bomb refugees
with food, and a few more perish
under the crashing crates of manna.

> Blowflies buzz, such bliss!
> Dogs grow fatter than ever.

Experts jet in—medical, forensic.
They distribute white suits,
surgical masks, and white gloves.

> Refugees are being immunized.
> The water they drink is purified.

Bright yellow bulldozers belch
black clouds of diesel smoke,
digging the bottomless trench.

> All down the river sun-bleached limbs dance.
> Little Brother, which leg is yours?

Exiles smile to be home, harvest
beans the refugees planted.
These new citizens patrol old borders.

Vultures cluck, such joy!
Hyenas giggle, fatter than ever.

The dead are aligned, so many
fenceposts, each wrapped and tied
in mats living women weave: dead banana leaves.

A million eat charity, injected
with health. The river water is purified.

Pairs of white-suited workers pitch
bodies into the trench, a layer
of wrapped bodies, a layer of lime.

All down the river torsos swell.
Little Brother, which belly is yours?

Perched at trench edge, separate
abacus beads strung on kilometers of wire,
experts count one million.

Maggots bloom out of bellies.
Crows whet beaks on bones, such glee!

Relief workers distribute plastic tents.
Defeated soldiers dance
round fires of food crates.

An army is being immunized.
The river it drinks has been purified.

Generals speak. Refugees listen,
held hostage at gunpoint,
planning the counterattack.

Exiles are being immunized.
The water they drink is purified.

One million flee for their lives
again. Their army on the run,
refugees would rather die at home.

Blowflies have never known such love.
Vultures are fatter than ever.

Grass grows over the airstrip. Grass grows
over the grave. And here come herdsmen
driving cows to pasture, never so green.

All down the river severed heads sing.
Little Brother, which song is yours?

Waking Again

He woke beneath the bodies of his friends
and couldn't tell which blood was his.
Here is Hell, they say. How does it begin

and who sent soldiers to shoot him when
he became a name on someone's list?
He woke beneath the bodies of his friends,

and clawed up through them until night
became morning, and limped past the hiss
of mortar shells. Who knows how he begins

to breathe again, past dying once?
His letter says how senseless it seemed
to wake beneath the bodies of his friends,

then go on living while his father's skin
dried tight to bones dogs gnawed. The ghosts
of war can say how it begins,

stuff fingers in each bullet hole to stem
the flood lead loosened over this
man, waking beneath bodies of his friends.
Maybe he can say how history ends.

Remera Arrives
Houston, Texas

Oh my God what I have done?
The climate, it is very hot here.
All people, where they are?

I hear four millions living here.
But I see no persons walking.
There are many cars. All people have one.

Inside the house it is so cold.
They call that conditioning air.
Mostly all people stay inside.

Derick is grown fat and ballhead.
And me too, I am fat now.
During the war, I almost starved to die.

But now I let grow my dreadlocks.
You must to have papers here before anything.
That is same for my country.

Food here is fake. Everythings puts in cans.
Cheeseburger is not real food.
The air smells like *l'essence.* Barbeque is OK.

For Fourth July they explode bombs
over the city, like back home
in Kigali on Liberation Day.

Me, I am learning slowly English.
Here all people say Howdy to mean greetings.
They smile at all the times. That is fake too.

Remera's Story

I am coming from Rwanda.

A tiny country in the middle of Africa.

My country became very famous and popular since 1994 by
    genocide in my country. Because we kill each other.

I would like to share with you my experiences in there in the
    genocide in my country.

Between April and June more than one million people were killed
    in my country.

I'd like to talk about genocide now.

What is the genocide?

The genocide in my country result in the massacre of more than
    one million.

I am someone of the survivor in my country.

In April 1994 I lost all my family and again my friends.

That is why I am here.

I'm trying to get my status of refugees and try to make my life in
    peace.

Anyway.

One week I stay to my home with all my family.

We don't know what we have to do.

 I remember my father say:

"If we try to escape from here to go to the church, maybe we'll be
    safe."

And then it was kind of confusing.

We don't know what was go on at that time.

And we decide if we stay together, we going to die together.

Maybe if we are separate, one of them can be save.

And then I left my home with my sister and my brother.

And we left our parents there.

On our road, my brother and my sister, we walk about 20 days.
Because we can't take the bus, we can't ride whatever means of
transportation.
We have to climb the mountain and travel all night in the forest.
And one day 21st April we was arrested by military on the
checkpoint.

When you are in that kind of situation you try to make something
to help you.
We erase the ethnie and we write we are Hutu.
But physically we are not Hutu.
That is the difference.
They say Tutsis have a long nose and Hutu a short nose.
That is fit for me.
And then they catch us and they ask:
"Who are you? Where are you going?"

Ah.
It was difficult to answer that.
Anyway.
They take us in the forest and they shoot us.
My little brother died at the same time.
And my sister after.
And me, I was shoot.
The military thought I was going die like my family.

In our way I saw a lot of things.
Death bodies who was eaten by dogs.
And in my mind I say if I stay in this forest I gonna die and then I'll
be eat by dogs.
Let me get out of this forest maybe someone will find me.
Maybe if I die on the road I'll be transported somewhere where
they put all people.

By chance, one of my friends who work in Butare find me and lead
me to the hospital.

As soon as I get to the hospital the militia came to kill people in
    that hospital.
Some of my friends was in hospital to work there.
And then they hide me again.

Three days after I can't support that.
I have to be get some medicine to try to moderate my wounds.
In that time I remember there was a woman from Belgium who
    was in the hospital.
I am her last patient.

She said:
"I'm sorry.
I can't spend all my time to you and as soon as I finish, you'll be
    killed on my eyes.
I can't."
And she give up.
But my friends try to help me.

At that time government say they have to let all Zairian citizens go
    back in their country.
And I pay some military to let me go in that convoy to Zaire.
That's why I escaped from Kigali the capital, from the university to
    the border.
I pay money and then I get to the border.

But as soon as I get to the border, I couldn't pass because I wasn't
    Zairian citizen.
And they say:
"No for you.
You have to stay in your country."

And then I spent two days in the bushes and when I feel strong.
Between my country and Zaire we have Lake Kivu as border.
And then I swim in the lake to Zaire.
I guess I was save.

But a few days after the RPF took my country in June.

And then those Hutu and military and former government have to
leave the country.

And again I was with those people who want to kill me in my
country.

And I can't support that.

As someone escape from Rwanda I couldn't feel well in that kind of
situation.

And then I decide if I have to die again, why not die in my own
country.

And then I decide to get back in my country.

But by the time since, change and change.